MORRIS
COMMERCIAL
V E H I C L E S

Harry Edwards

SUTTON PUBLISHING

First published in the United Kingdom in 1992 by
Alan Sutton Publishing Limited
Phoenix Mill · Far Thrupp · Stroud · Gloucestershire

First published in the United States of America in 1992 by
Alan Sutton Publishing Inc · Wolfeboro Falls · NH 03896–0848

British Library Cataloguing in Publication Data

Edwards, Harry
Morris Commerical Vehicles
I. Title
629.223

ISBN 0-7509-0176-4

Library of Congress Cataloging in Publication Data applied for

Typeset in 10/12 Palatino.
Typesetting and origination by
Alan Sutton Publishing Limited.
Printed in Great Britain by
WBC, Bridgend, Mid Glam.

INTRODUCTION

'Morris' as a make of motor car dates back to the early days of 1913 when the first production Morris Oxford left the old military academy building at Temple Cowley, outside
Oxford, which served as Morris's original works. Perhaps 'assembly plant' would be a
better description, as those early Morris cars were, in fact, assembled from a multitude of
proprietary parts made elsewhere. For example, the wheels came from Sankey, the tyres
from Dunlop, radiators from Doherty Motor Components Ltd, White & Poppe made the
engines, and from the same firm came the gearboxes, clutches and carburettors. For the
carbide lamps Morris turned to Powell & Hanmer; to Germany for the Bosch magneto
and spark plugs, and to Belgium for the chassis frames. The Birmingham-based firm of
E.G. Wrigley & Co. supplied the front and rear axle assemblies from their factory at
Foundry Lane, Soho.

Within a year of the introduction of the Morris Oxford light car, a commercial derivative was being listed, but these were made only in very small numbers. It was not until
1924 that a serious attempt to capture some of the light van market was made with the
introduction of the 8 cwt van based on the contemporary Morris Cowley 11.9 hp chassis.
From then on, with modifications each season, the Morris light van became very popular
with small traders. The adoption of the Morris light van by the General Post Office as
their workhorse did much to boost sales so that by the late 1920s these light commercials
were to be seen everywhere.

Meanwhile, William Richard Morris was looking to compete in the slightly heavier
commercial market which, at that time, was dominated by substantial imports and
home-based competitors such as the Manchester assembled Ford Model-T one-tonner.
The answer came when, at the end of 1923, the one-time supplier of parts to Morris,
E.G. Wrigley & Co. Ltd, went into liquidation. Morris purchased the large works with its
modern machine equipment from the Receivers for £213, 044. Initially trading as 'W.R.
Morris, Successor to E.G. Wrigley & Co. Ltd', the Foundry Lane Works became 'Morris
Commercial Cars Ltd' in February 1924.

The first Morris Commercial to be produced was the T-type one-tonner using the well-
tried 13.9 hp 'Hotchkiss'-type side-valve engine as fitted to the contemporary Morris
Oxford car. The first such T-type left the production line in May 1924 and by the end of
that year 2, 487 tonners had been assembled.

From that time the range of Morris Commercials expanded. Variations of the tonner
came in van, bus and ambulance form, then a light tonner and a 12 cwt van, also utilizing
the car type engine, were introduced. In 1926 a purpose-built engine of 15.9 hp was
designed for use in the new Z-type 25 cwt model, and this engine found a use in the TX-
and R-type 30 cwt vehicles which followed. From the R-type was derived a six-wheeler
D-type used in the inter-war period in great numbers by the British Army.

Heavy Morris Commercials came in 1930 when the company produced the 2½ ton

P-type Leader (later uprated to 3 tons), followed a year later by the J-type Courier which came as a 4 ton normal control or a 5 ton forward control chassis. The total output of J-types was small, accounting for 112 units between 1931 and 1934.

A move by Morris Commercial Cars Ltd from Foundry Lane, Soho, to Adderley Park in 1932 coincided with a further increase in the range of models and the first venture by Morris into the double-deck bus market with his HD-type Imperial. Single-deck bus chassis had previously been made in the shape of the normal control Y-type Viceroy and the forward control and normal control versions of the Dictator H-type chassis.

Morris Commercial was one of the first large British motor manufacturers to enter the taxi-cab field following a change in the regulations governing the design of cabs in 1927. Announced in January 1929, the first of these was the Morris Commercial Type-G International which, in turn, was superseded in 1932 by the G2 Junior with a four-cylinder engine and the G2S Junior six-cylinder version. The later G2SW Super Six taxis followed in 1937 and continued in production until the Second World War. Thereafter the Nuffield Wolseley Oxford taxi-cab catered for this market.

A change in policy by Morris Commercial Cars Ltd was seen in 1933 when they announced a new range of vehicles to be known as the C-types. Using a high percentage of common parts throughout the range, the C-types, in both four- and six-cylinder form, ranged from 30 cwt to 5 tons. This approach, with its sub-division of normal and forward control, was obviously a success for in 1937 the new CV, or 'Equi-load', series was introduced and continued to be manufactured for the civilian market up to the outbreak of war in 1939. After the war, when production resumed, the six-cylinder version was dropped. When Morris Commercial entered the diesel engine market in 1948 a 5 ton six-cylinder diesel version, known as the ECVO, was offered.

For a short period of about a year, starting in January 1950, Morris Commercial re-entered the PSV market with the OP-type forward control coach powered by a six-cylinder diesel engine of 4256 cc. The following month the same design was offered with a 3770 cc petrol engine, designated the PP-type. In June 1950 the diesel version was fitted with a larger 4459 cc engine, but the coaches ceased to be listed after September 1951.

Although light vans in the form of derivatives of Morris cars continued to be made by Morris Motors at Cowley, similar rated vehicles were made by Morris Commercial. The 10 cwt J-type van, first introduced in 1949 with a 1470 cc side-valve engine coupled via a three-speed gearbox, was later updated as the JB-type with a larger overhead-valve (or ohv) Austin B-series 1489 cc engine and a four-speed gearbox in 1957. In 1960 came the replacement model for the earlier J-type with its chassis frame, the new petrol engined J4 model (later known as the J4 M10) of mono-construction in van or pick-up form. Two years later a diesel engined option was available. The J2 (later renamed as J2 M16) was a 15 cwt vehicle which followed a similar evolution as the 10 cwt, but was available from the outset in 1956 as van, pick-up, or minibus. Starting with an ohv four-cylinder 1489 cc engine in 1956, the option of a diesel was added in 1961; then a larger 1622 cc petrol engine in 1963, and an automatic gearbox in 1964. The designation 'J3' does not figure in this look at the J models, but such a vehicle was actually planned, based on the J4 model but with a 948 cc A-series engine. However, it never went into production. In January 1967 an underfloor engined petrol or diesel version with a longer wheelbase, called the 250 JU, could be purchased as a van, pick-up or bus.

An earlier 15/20 cwt Morris Commercial van with a forward control cab and called the PV was generally available when production resumed after the war, but its pre-war design with wood-framed body gave a clue to the fact that just over fifty of these vehicles had been made before the war. Some 15,500 of these were made before production ceased in 1953.

The successor to the PV was the 1 ton LD-type first available in July 1952. Like the PV this was a forward control van with a traditional wood-framed body and had a four-cylinder ohv petrol engine. It continued in this form until 1960 when the model was re-designated LD1. Meanwhile a 2.2 litre version had been added in 1955. In 1960 the LD4-type, with a larger petrol engine, and the LD04 type, with a 2.2 litre diesel engine, super-seded the early version. Both models were renamed as LD M20 in 1962 and then as 260 LD in 1968.

The LD2-type was the larger 1½ ton version available from 1953 onwards and two years later the LD02, a 2.2 litre diesel, made its appearance. Both were superseded in 1960 as the LD5 and LD05 respectively, and each had 2.2 litre engines, with four-speed synchromesh gearboxes. In 1964 an ambulance chassis with a choice of either petrol or diesel was listed.

Part of the CV or Equi-load range mentioned earlier was the 25/30 cwt LC model. With various modifications in design the LC continued in production from its inception in 1937 to the early 1960s. The LC started with a 15.9 hp (2050 cc) ohv engine as van or truck, continued between 1948 to 1952 in a slightly modified form as the LC3 (there was no LC2 model), then with a longer wheelbase as the LC4-type for a year in 1952/3. When superseded in 1953 the LC5, in truck form only, had a shorter stroke 2199 cc engine fit-ted. This was the Austin 2.2 litre four-cylinder version of the Austin six-cylinder D-series which had been introduced by Austin in 1948, now available to Morris Commercial after the amalgamation of Austin and Morris. This engine was to become universal in all LD and LC models. Complementary to the LC5 was the LC05 which was a four-cylinder diesel version.

The LC variations came to an end in February 1960 when a new design, the S.200 series forward control truck was introduced. This truck had the option of a four-cylinder petrol or 2.2 litre diesel engine. To complicate matters the model designation was changed from the S.200 series in January 1962 to 'FG.K30', then in January 1968 it was renamed the '360.FG'-type. The reasoning behind the type title changes were two-fold. 'FG.K30' indi-cated that the vehicle had a 'FG' style cab, built at Bathgate, Scotland, denoted by the let-ter 'K', and had a 30 cwt payload. The second change in designation reflected the changes made in classification, giving gross vehicle weight instead of payload. Hence '360.FG' meant 3.6 tons gross vehicle weight and the FG-type cab.

An export-only version, the S.203 series (WE.K30), as chassis and normal control cab, was exported from 1961. Various options were available, namely 2.2 litre four-cylinder pertrol, six-cylinder petrol (this was the Austin D-series mentioned above), 2.2 litre or 3.4 litre diesel; the latter being replaced by a 3.8 litre diesel engine in 1963. When the WF.K30 model (renamed 360.WF in 1968) was finally released to the home market in July 1964 it was with a redesigned WF cab which had a single piece windscreen and was the first Morris Commercial to have four horizontally mounted headlights.

Heavy Morris Commercials in the Series III range began production early in 1955. The 3 ton version, in forward control as 303.FC, and the normal control model 303.NC, had the option of petrol or diesel engine. Later, with modifications, the model type was renamed WF.K60 for the normal control, and then in January 1968 as 600WF. The for-ward control version of the three-tonner was superseded by Series IV (304) with six-cylinder petrol engine or four-cylinder diesel and the new style FG cab in 1959 (later designated FG.K60, then 550.FG). The Series III four-tonner followed a similar parttern, starting as the 403.NC (normal control) and 403.FC (forward control), later replaced by the Series IV (404.FG), this, in turn, being called the FG.K80 then 700.FG. For the five-tonner the Series III (503.NC) became known as the WE.K100, then 830 WF, in normal control, while the forward control versions Series III (503.FC) later took the identification

Series IV (504), then FF.K100. Two other 5 ton Morris Commercials were available in the early sixties; the FG.K100 Low Loader which had a re-designed cab with angled door and low set corner windows, and the FH.K100 (FH was an FF cab modified) which had an underfloor diesel engine, later replaced by the FJ.K100. There was no 6 ton version in the Series III range but vehicles of this rating came in 1962 with the normal control WE.K120, subsequently replaced by the WF.K120 with twin headlights and a one piece windscreen, later renamed 1050.WF. The 7 ton Series III, called the 701 model, had a forward control 'FE' cab, power steering, and a two-speed Eaton axle as standard. Long wheelbase, short wheelbase, and tipper versions were available. The replacements for these models were the Series IV (702) or FF.K140, and later the FH.K140 and the underfloor engined diesel FJ.K140 (redesignated 1160.FJ). Prime Movers in the Series III series started with the 503 FC in petrol or diesel form and were superseded by the Series IV (504) in 1958. Other Prime Movers to follow on were the FF.K240 with a GTW of 12 tons, FF.K300 (GTW 15 tons), FF.K340 (17 tons), and FF.K360 (18 tons). The FJ versions with underfloor diesel were the FJ.K240 (12 tons), FJ.K300 (15 tons), FJ.K340 (17 tons), and the FJ.K360 (later renamed 1800 FJT).

When the interests of Austin Motor Company and the Nuffield Organization were merged in 1952 to form the British Motor Corporation Ltd it inherited duplicate outlets for various types of vehicles. To cater for both Austin and Morris franchises the short-term answer was in badge engineering where identical models were simply Morris or Austin by virtue of the badge. This was no less true for new commercial models, resulting in the same design differing by type designation as well as badge. An attempt at rationalization was made in 1962 when all Austin and Morris commercials of the same type were given a common type number, accounting for some of the designation changes mentioned above. This proved to be the prelude to a major change which took place in August 1968, when it was announced that badge engineering was to cease and all Austin and Morris commercials were to be marketed under the BMC symbol. 'Morris Commercial' had come to an end.

MORRIS CAR-DERIVED VANS (CDVs)

Production of light vans based on the contemporary Morris Cowley car chassis were first produced in any quantity in 1924, fitted with a flattened version of the 'bullnose' radiator, unique to the vans.

Illustrated here are 1926 season versions of the 8 cwt Standard and the 8 cwt De luxe vans. Both versions utilized the 11.9 hp side-valve engine with a bore of 69.5 mm and a stroke of 102 mm coupled to a three-speed gearbox via, on the early versions, a four plate cork insert clutch running in oil.

The double loading doors at the rear were common to both models but on the Standard van the driver was obliged to enter via the single half-door on the nearside. On the De Luxe version two half-doors were provided and to achieve this the spare wheel was moved to the rear end of the running board. On the more expensive model additional equipment in the form of a roof-rack and sliding doors behind the driver's seat was provided.

Although, being based on the car chassis, the wings, lamps and aprons etc. were finished in black, the main bodywork was always supplied in shop-grey primer to enable the customer to arrange final livery colour after delivery.

Half-way between commercial and car was the Morris Cowley Commercial Traveller's Car which was first introduced in 1925 and continued to be listed, first in 'bullnose' and later in 'flatnose' form, until 1929. The basic bodywork was that of the two-seater Cowley with the addition of a box body at the rear intended for a traveller's samples. In this 1925 example, supplied by Bonallack & Sons of Romford, Essex, purpose-built drawers and a security Yale lock have been added. The price of £205 for this specialist vehicle can be compared with £198 for the standard Cowley 11.9 hp two-seater.

A surviving example of the 'bullnose' Morris Cowley Commercial Traveller's Car of 1925.

Rear view of the 1928 model 10 cwt light van based on the Morris Cowley chassis. Front wheel braking was standard and the driver's doors were fitted with winding windows. Note the 'four wheel brakes' inverted triangle around the single rear lamp.

Controls and instrumentation on the Morris light vans were similar to those on the Cowley car, as shown here for the 1927 model tourer.

Most of the CDVs were based on the Morris Cowley chassis in the twenties. One exception was the 'Traveller's Brougham', which made use of the 1928 Morris Oxford 14/28 hp car chassis. Priced at £255, the vehicle was available in blue, maroon or brown and provided 'exceptional facilities for the orderly disposal of a multitude of goods or samples'.

By 1929 the capacity of the Morris light van, now rated as 8/10 cwt, had been increased by dint of lowering the side panels below the rear mudguards, as shown on this 1930 model.Although the 'bullnose' radiator on the cars had been superseded by the flat radiator in late 1926, the vans continued to be fitted with, what later became known as, the 'squashed bullnose' radiator. A short version of this curious radiator was fitted on the earlier 1924–6 versions. Front wheel brakes, which had been offered as an option on the 1927 vans, became standard fitting the following year.

The MORRIS LIGHT VAN
(8-cwt.)

The 'flatnose' radiator was finally incorporated into the van design for the 1931 season. The rest of the design had been adopted from the earlier models, but introduced curvature to the roof of the driver's cab on this model. The bodywork of these small commercials was made up of steel panels on a wood frame with Plymax used for the van body. Since the previous year, all bright parts had been chromium plated and Triplex safety glass was fitted as standard. A major change was that a modified version of the larger 13.9 hp Oxford car engine had been substituted for the smaller 11.9 hp unit.

A typical example of the so-called 'Hotchkiss' 11.9 and 13.9 hp side-valve engines used in the Morris light vans. Although generally known by enthusiasts as the 'Hotchkiss' type, these engines were of Morris manufacture. The misnomer resulted from the fact that the first of these engines was made by Hotchkiss et Cie of Coventry before the firm was taken over by Morris to become their engines branch.

6

Once a Morris light van, this chassis was given a new lease of life as the focus of Rudi Wallenda's clowning act. Clever modifications allow the doors to fall off, headlamps to swivel, front mudguards to fold up suddenly, steering wheel to become detached, and the engine to 'explode'. (R. Wallenda)

The appearance of the 1932 van was almost identical to the previous year, with the exception of the deletion of the oval side windows behind the doors, which had been increased in width. A complete redesign of the bodywork was undertaken for the 1933 season (as shown) with a more rounded appearance, particularly with regard to the front wings. Morris Motors Ltd tended to base the van on components used in the car chassis of the previous season; however, in this instance the wings and the three-stud steel artillery wheels had been phased out on the Cowley car at the end of the 1931 season.

The 1934 8/10 cwt van had a longer wheelbase (105 in) than the contemporary Cowley car but had caught up in other respects, the most noticeable change being the use of Magna wire wheels. Not so obvious, until driven, was the introduction of hydraulic braking. The vehicle illustrated is a modified van supplied by Bonallack & Sons to the Borough of Poplar Electricity Department for display purposes. For the first time, Morris Motors Ltd were offering the 8/10 cwt van in other than shop grey. At extra cost the customer could choose the options of blue, black, brown or green cellulose finish.

In mid-1935 the replacement for the 8/10 cwt van came as a complete redesign, specifically as a light commercial. This, the Series II 10 cwt semi-forward drive, was available with van or truck bodywork. Interesting features of this new model were the off-set engine, which allowed sufficient leg room for the driver, and dissimilar track front and rear (50 and 54 in respectively). Curiously, despite incorporating many up-to-date features such as the self-cancelling semaphore indicators and stowage for the spare wheel behind the number plate panel, the designers opted for a centre accelerator pedal.

Early models were fitted with mud shields over the Magna wire wheels at the rear. Later models were to be changed to the Easiclean disc type.

On the truck version, in order to anticipate amendments to lighting regulations and avoid obscuring the rear number plate when the tailboard was lowered at night, an additional number plate and tail lamp were provided which utilized two hooks to fit over the upper edge of the tailboard when down, the lamp being plugged into a socket provided.

The small truck version of the Series II Morris 10 cwt van was put on the market in June 1938. The truck sides and tailboard, made of T&G timber, were detachable after removing the canvas tilt and hoops.

The Series II 10 cwt ceased production in late 1939 and the announcement of its successor coincided with the early days of the Second World War, in the 'phoney war' period. As a result, few of the new Series Y vans were to reach the civilian market until production resumed after the war in 1945.

The Series Y 10 cwt, mainly in van form, although a few truck versions were made in 1940, used the same off-set 11.9 hp engine as its predecessor but the earlier coachbuilt bodywork had been replaced with an all steel construction. All steel, that is, with the exception of the roof which was of the traditional leathercloth over timber lath design.

The General Post Office were the main fleet users of the new Series Y vans, which had a production period of ten years. During this decade the GPO took delivery of 34,117 vans for postal use and 605 for telephone engineers.

During the Second World War a long wheelbase version of the Morris Series Y was manufactured for military use as an ambulance. Many body pressings from the civilian van were used but on the military vehicles a larger 14 hp side-valve engine replaced the 11.9 hp unit. Another feature was the smaller diameter wheels with low-pressure tyres. (L. Orton)

An example of swords into plough-shares is this ex-military Series Y ambulance at present in use in Sri Lanka. (K. Martin)

To replace the Series Y 10 cwt van, Morris Motors Ltd resurrected the name 'Cowley' in 1950 for the Series MCV pick-up and van, which had front end treatment based on the contemporary 1476 cc Morris Oxford MO car.

In turn the MCV model gave way in September 1956 to a replacement, the Series III Morris half-ton which lasted until 1962, when the next contender for the 20 cwt market was a light commercial derived from the Austin A55 car. Austin and Morris had by this time been amalgamated as the British Motor Corporation for ten years. The example shown here is a 1961 Series III half-ton with milk float bodywork by Osborne & Son Ltd of Saffron Walden, Essex.

A caravan conversion of the M/HV4 van with a dual personality, carrying both Austin and Morris badges.

The Morris-badged counterpart of the Austin A55 commercial, in either van or pick-up form, was the Morris half-ton introduced in late 1962 as types M/HV4 and M/HK4.

Within twelve months of the little 8 hp Morris Minor arriving on the scene in 1928 to compete with the Austin Seven, its chassis was used to create a 5 cwt van, making it one of the first, if not the only, production ohc engined small commercial. By 1931 most of the Morris Minor car variants had gone side-valve and the van followed suit. Unlike the car version, which by 1932 had undergone design changes, including the relocation of the petrol tank from under the bonnet to the rear, the van was to continue to rely on a gravity feed system until the 1934 season. It did, however, retain the small rectangular flat radiator and 'boxed' mudguards throughout its production period which came to an end in 1934.

A few small fire engines were made by Morris Motors Ltd on the 1931 ohv Minor chassis. These were advertised as being suitable for villages, factories, schools, institutions, etc. Morris Cowley Works used one, and it is known that both the Oxford Fire Brigade and the fire brigade at Worthing used these machines. At least one is known to have been exported to India for use by the Maharaj Rana Bahadure of Jhalawar. No water pump was fitted, the fire fighting equipment comprised about nine large fire extinguishers and adjustable ladders. The bell was the normal warning device fitted to all fire engines of the period.

As the method of construction for the early cars entailed mounting the complete body on a separate running chassis, it was a simple matter later to convert this to a small commercial, such as this little truck based on the Morris Minor.

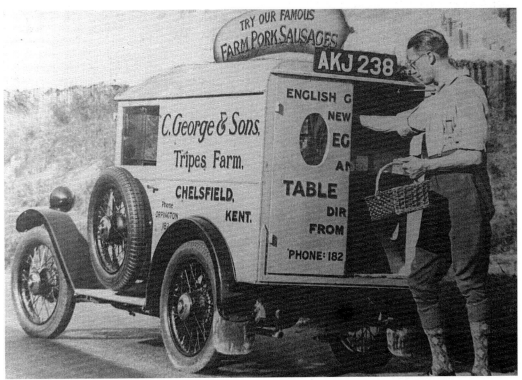

Externally the side-valve engined version of the Morris Minor van was almost identical to the earlier ohv version. Only on closer inspection were differences apparent. On this 1933 example Magna wire wheels were fitted and the side or parking lights had been combined within the headlamp units. (C. George)

The 1931 under bonnet arrangement of the four-cylinder 847 cc Morris Minor side-valve engine. The filler cap for the gravity feed scuttle-mounted petrol tank and the Lucas 'Sparton' horn are visible in this view

The final version of the Morris Minor 5 cwt van was available for the 1934 season, when attempts were made to round off the severe corners of the earlier body design. The gravity feed scuttle-mounted fuel tank had been replaced with a tank at the rear in conjunction with an electric petrol pump. Despite the adoption of a hydraulic braking system on the 1934 season cars, the van design retained the cable-operated arrangement using a system of pulleys as illustrated.

The General Post Office took delivery of a number of 5 cwt Morris Minor vans from early 1932. These had bodies built to a GPO design on a standard Minor van chassis. The introduction of the Morris Eight, in 1934, spawned a curious hybrid built to the GPO specification by a number of proprietary bodybuilders on a Minor chassis, which had been mated to many Morris Eight components including the 918 cc engine. The single-piece front mudguards and the radiator used were of the type fitted to the last of the Morris Minors.

Three types of van were produced: the postal van, finished in red and having a basic van body with sloping roof over the cab; the engineers internal van was similar, but finished in green, and was for use by telephone engineers servicing telephone equipment; the third, and most interesting, was the engineers external van, which carried an extending ladder on the roof and an additional angled green window above the windscreen to allow the telephone engineer to view roadside telephone lines while seated in the cab. Examples of this latter type and the postal van are shown.

The most successful Morris vehicle of the 1930s was the Morris Eight, which made its debut at London's Olympia Motor Show in October 1934. The specification of the Morris Eight 5 cwt van was almost identical to the car and included a newly designed 918 cc side-valve engine and Lockheed hydraulic brakes. However, the car-type bumpers and running boards were not fitted and, while the car had 17 in Magna wire wheels, the van wheels were small hub-type wire wheels with 18 in diameter tyres.

When, eventually, the Morris Eight car was updated to the Series II model with a modified radiator shell and Easiclean wheels in 1937, the van continued as before, right up to the outbreak of war in 1939, by which time the car version had been out of production for a year, superseded by the Series E Morris Eight.

The Morris Eight 5 cwt van not only provided the ideal transport for small businesses such as grocers, fishmongers, dry cleaners, and the like, but also went to make up larger fleets such as the adapted versions used by the *Manchester Evening News* publishers. The open apertures in the sides allowed bundles of the latest edition to be quickly passed to the waiting newsagent. Prior to the use of the small Morris vans, the *Manchester Evening News*, and its now defunct competitor, the *Manchester Evening Chronicle*, relied on high-wheeled horse-drawn gigs for speedy delivery.

Inside the cab of the Morris Eight 5 cwt van. The instruments, grouped on a small centre panel, were fairly comprehensive and included an ammeter, oil pressure gauge, petrol gauge and throttle adjustment. The single blade windscreen wiper was driven by the 'spin-to-start' motor above the adjustable windscreen.

The easily accessible 918 cc side-valve engine as fitted to the Morris Eight 5 cwt vans. Unlike the earlier Morris Minor vans, the radiator filler cap was now to be found under the bonnet. Other features shown here are the SU electric petrol pump mounted on the front of the felt-lined tool box, the large 4½ in diameter Lucas dynamo and the SU carburettor.

Posed against the background of the Danish royal palace, this unique Morris Eight 5 cwt van chassis with advertising body in light blue was designed by Mr Wodschow, sales manager of the Danish Morris agents, Messrs Vilh Nelleman, in conjunction with Chr Friis, for the latter's coffee import business. The bodywork was made in Copenhagen.

Brake bodywork built on a Series I Morris Eight car chassis by an unknown coachbuilder, around 1938.

Concurrent with the Series Y Morris 10 cwt, the 5 cwt van, called the Morris Eight Series Z, also appeared on the scene in the early days of the Second World War. While this can be loosely considered to be the commercial derivative of the Series E Morris Eight as it shared the same basic 918 cc engine, the front and bonnet configuration and a common wheelbase (7 ft 5 in) with dissimilar track dimensions giving a wider track at the rear, there were many features unique to the van. Unlike its predecessor, the Series I Morris Eight van, which utilized the same engine, gearbox, dashboard arrangement, radiator type, etc., as its car equivalent, the Series Z had its own radiator surround design, an all steel body mounted on a separate chassis, and a different dashboard arrangement which made use of the earlier Morris Eight instruments. Also borrowed from the earlier Eight was the three-speed gearbox, albeit mated to the later engine.

The General Post Office used thousands of these Series Z vans for both postal and telephone duties. Apart from a small number from the earliest batch, the GPO did not insist on their own design of coachbuilt bodies but settled for the standard Morris body with modifications to fittings such as 'railway carriage' type door handles, battery cut-out switch, lockable tool box, wood dash and door capping, external bonnet catches, petrol tank stone guards, and integral hub caps on the Easiclean wheels, etc.

Many Morris chassis, both car and commercial, were supplied to contemporary coachbuilders for special purpose-built bodywork. This example is of a Series Z 8 hp 5 cwt chassis with van bodywork by Bray's Coachbuilders of Leicester, dating from 1950. (J. Lord)

The first completely new post-war Morris car was the very successful Morris Minor designed by the late Sir Alec Issigonis. In its early form the Minor car had a modified version of the 918 cc side-valve engine carried on from the Series E Morris Eight. By 1953 the revised model had taken on an 803 cc ohv engine, but it was not until the introduction of this model (known as the Series II) that a commercial derivative appeared, to replace the Series Z van. In its commercial guise the Morris Minor O-type was initially rated at 5 cwt as van or pick-up, until 1962 when both rating and engine was upgraded to 6 cwt with a 1098 cc engine. During the production of the 6 cwt, a heavier 8 cwt version was also marketed from 1968. Morris Minor O-type light commercials ceased production in late 1971, but not before they had become the mainstay of the GPO light van fleet.

This Series MM Morris Minor was specially converted as a 'one-off' into a fire engine for the works' fire brigade at Morris Motors Ltd, Cowley.

The introduction of the Morris Mini in 1959 – and still in production today, albeit with a simple 'Mini' badge – provided another basis for a small CDV. The 5 cwt van version was put on the market in June 1960 – the month this example was registered in Buckinghamshire.

Carrying either Austin or Morris badges, the 7 and 10 cwt vans derived from the Morris Marina car were officially announced in August 1972 as a replacement for the Morris Minor based van. For the 7 cwt payload version there was an option of the BLMC 'A' series power unit of 1100 cc or the larger 1300 cc engine, combined with standard or deluxe trim. These 7 cwt vans used the semi-floating Triumph rear axle and gearbox. The larger engine was also fitted to the 10 cwt De Luxe van and while this van also made use of the Triumph gearbox its rear axle was a BMC 3/4 floating design. When first introduced it was available in Glacier White, Green Mallard, Teal Blue, Harvest Gold or Skymist Grey. In all models the upholstery was navy blue. Although up-dated in line with the changes made to the Morris Marina car, and subsequently with its 1980 successor the Morris Ital, this was to prove to be the last of the car-derived vans to carry the Morris badge. In 1983 the name became motoring history.

MORRIS COMMERCIALS

William Morris took over the factory of E.G. Wrigley & Co. Ltd, at Soho, Birmingham, in 1924 and commenced trading as Morris Commercial Cars Ltd at the beginning of the following year. No time was lost in designing the first Morris Commercial for by May 1924 the first one-tonner T-type was completed.

In its original form the tonner utilized the well tried 'Hotchkiss'-type four-cylinder side-valve engine being used in the Morris Oxford of the period. Brakes were fitted only to the rear wheels and, in the manner of the contemporary car, the clutch was a Morris design with cork inserts running in oil.

The first vehicle to be produced has survived (above) and is now part of the British Motor Industry Heritage Trust collection. Note the single word 'MORRIS' cast into the radiator header tank.

Another example of the early T-type one-tonner is this lorry used by H. Tuckwell & Sons Ltd of Oxford. The sparse lighting set comprised the large side lamps and a single tail light, although a 'five lamp system' could be had as an extra.

The one-tonner Morris Commercial chassis was soon a very popular basis for the many commercial bodybuilders of the time, with interesting results, such as this van with a severe rear overhang made for Batger & Co. Ltd of London for transportation of their confectionary products.

This purpose-built newspaper van, for the *London Evening News*, was based on the 1928 T-type tonner chassis. The plated radiator shell shown here, in place of the standard cast aluminium radiator, was normally fitted to special ambulance and shooting brake versions of the tonner.

This 1929 T-type one-tonner, which was used by the Government Instructional Centre for the unemployed, illustrates the later adoption of full length doors giving the driver some weather protection. Note also the later type aluminium radiator with 'Morris Commercial' cast in full on the header tank. By now the louvres on the top of the bonnet, a feature of the early T-types, had gone.

A range of T-type vans were supplied complete by Morris Commercial including the Standard van which came equipped with 'three lamp electric lighting' – two small front lamps and a rear light. At this time most commercials provided scant protection for the driver, and Morris Commercials were no exception; all vans had simple half-doors to the cab. Shown here are the Standard van (above) and the De Luxe van (below). Opposite are the Special Furniture van (above) and the Special Bakers van (below).

33

The first major change in design of the tonner came in 1931 when a new and larger radiator, with chromium plated shell, transformed the appearance. Now designated the T2-type, the mechanics of these early versions, made at Soho, were much the same as before, continuing the use of the 13.9 hp 'Hotchkiss'-type side-valve engine, rear wheel brakes only and, as yet, no bumpers. Wider tyres also contributed to the change in appearance. Both van and truck versions were available.

With the chromium-plated radiator surround, a new badge made its appearance with the words 'Morris Commercial' superimposed on a globe. Later versions of this badge would carry the company slogan 'British to the Backbone'. The Wilmot Breeden calormeter was not a standard fitment on the tonner, but could easily be purchased from a motor factor of the period for about £1, and provided a useful monitor of the water temperature in the radiator.

In late 1932 production of the T2 tonner was transferred to the new Morris Commercial works at Adderley Park, Birmingham, and with this move came a number of changes which were not readily apparent. Four-wheel brakes were now fitted as well as front bumpers, while under the bonnet the original magneto was replaced with a coil ignition system, and the mechanical tyre pump fitted to the early models was deleted from the specification

A new forward control alternative with van bodywork (T2F) was also added to the range at this time and, although the normal control vehicles still retained a scuttle-mounted petrol tank with gravity feed, the forward control versions had an 11 gallon tank mounted on the off-side of the chassis using an Autovac to feed the carburettor.

So far the narrative has concentrated on the tonner, but soon after the formation of the company Morris Commercial also began producing other models, both smaller and larger. The L-type, rated at 12 cwt, came on the scene first as a van then, around 1927, also in truck form. The L-type had a shorter wheelbase of 9 ft 6 in, compared with the tonner's 10 ft 2 in, and the smaller 11.9 hp 'Hotchkiss'-type car engine as fitted to the Morris Cowley car. Mechanically the L-type differed little in general construction to the T-type, although it had shorter springs with a modified shackle arrangement, narrower tyres, an open propeller shaft, and smaller 14 in diameter drums for the rear wheel braking system.

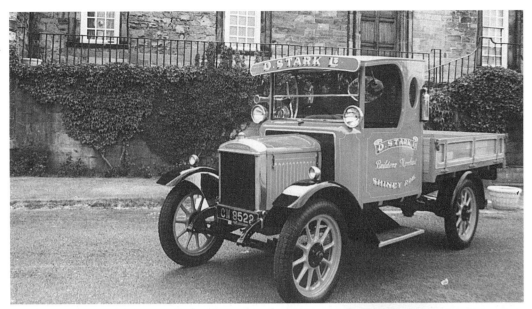

Another variation was the LT model, or light tonner, introduced in 1927. This was a curious mixture of the smaller 12 cwt L-type and the larger 1 ton T-type. It had the 13.9 hp engine and the larger 15 in diameter brake drums from the tonner, but followed the wheelbase dimensions of the L-type and had its open propeller shaft. It was not a successful model and was only produced between 1927 and 1930, during which period only just over 3,000 units were made. Illustrated here is a preserved example owned by Denis Stark of Tyne & Wear.

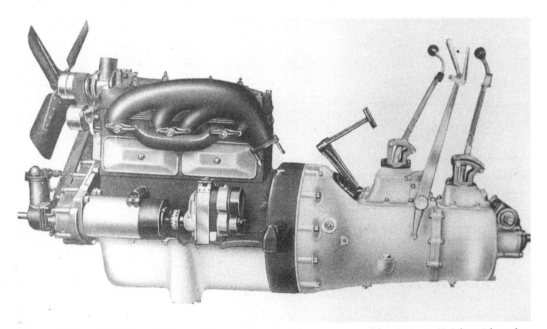

Up until the mid-1930s all Morris Commercials had been powered by 11.9 or 13.9 hp side-valve engines of the type used in the contemporary Morris cars. A decision was taken to design an engine specifically for the commercial vehicles and the result was the side-valve Z-type engine rated at 15.9 hp. A feature of the new engine was the arrangement of the Lucas magneto and dynamo in tandem on the near-side of the engine block with an extension of the drive to power a Maxwell air pump through its own gear clutch. The pump is shown here on the left of the photograph.

The first Morris Commercial to utilize the new Z-type engine was the 24 and 30 cwt Z-type of 1926, with a 10 ft 2 in wheelbase; a model which was to continue in production for two years. A longer wheelbase version (11 ft 6 in) with twin rear wheels was also available rated at 30 cwt, and as a PSV chassis. Dewandre vacuum servo operated four-wheel brakes were standard on the long wheelbase models such as the example illustrated here, which was used by J. Masters & Co. Ltd of Barking, Essex, who marketed the well-known Army & Navy matches. In total 7,181 Z-type commercials were made, including a few motor fire pumps on the shorter chassis which were designated the F-type.

F-type Morris Commercial fire pump supplied to Brightlingsea Urban District Council in 1930.

Off-side view of the Z-type four-cylinder side-valve engine. With a 85 mm bore and 125 mm stroke, the power unit was rated at 15.9 hp.

The second model to be produced at the Soho works using the Z-type engine was the TX-type which mainly superseded the Z-type. These were much heavier vehicles and were marketed initially as '30 cwt Super' models between 1928–9, but uprated to 35/40 cwt for the 1930 and 1931 seasons, with the option of 11 ft and 13 ft wheelbase. In 1931 a bored-out version of the Z-type engine, rated at 17.9 hp, gave the TX-type a more powerful power unit. Purchasers were now given the option of chassis with 11 ft, 13 ft, or 14 ft wheelbase. Ironically, these TX models all relied on rear wheel braking only and it was not until the 1932 and 1933 season's 'TX2', now rated at 45/50 cwt, that four-wheel braking was fitted. These, the last of the TX models, in short (11 ft) and long (14 ft) wheelbase, had twin rear wheels. Illustrated is the 35/40 cwt version.

A popular mode of holiday transport in the 1920s and early 1930s was the open charabanc. Here a TX based vehicle, owned by 'Coxs Car', has brought visitors to the Cheddar Gorge.

TX-type chassis being assembled on the Morris Commercial Cars Ltd assembly line at Soho, Birmingham, in the late 1920s.

A gap existed in the market between the T-type one-tonner and the heavier TX-type, especially after the latter had been uprated in the early 1930s. The answer came with the introduction in 1928 of the Morris Commercial R-type, initially called the '25 cwt Super' truck. Continuing the use of the Z-type 15.9 hp engine, the R-type was to undergo a number of changes during its five-year production period. In 1929 (now known as the 'Middleweight Champion') it was fitted with a four-speed gearbox and given a 30 cwt rating, although, as shown above in chassis form, braking was still restricted to the rear wheels.

A surviving example of a 1929 30 cwt R-type with ten-seater bus bodywork. (P.J. Reynolds)

Ambulances based on the Morris Commercial R-type, were listed as 'Standard' or 'De Luxe'. Prices ranged from £400 to £445 depending on the equipment supplied. The external finish was either brush grained or paint finish. Shown here is the De Luxe version.

R-type 30 cwt Morris Commercials between 1931 and 1933 had the wheelbase increased to 11 ft 2 in and, after a short production period with a larger 17.9 hp version of the Z-type engine, it was fitted with the same engine now bored-out yet again to rate at 19.2 hp. On these models front wheel brakes were added. Meanwhile, during the same period, two larger 2 ton 'Economy' models were introduced – 'R.11/40' having a 11 ft 2 in wheelbase (the model designation indicates this dimension together with the rating in hundredweights) and the 'R.13/40' with a wheelbase of 13 ft. A notable feature of the economy model was the introduction of a pressed-metal radiator surround replacing the, by now, traditional Morris Commercial cast aluminium radiator assembly. Between 1928 and 1933, when production of the R-type came to an end, some 17,745 left the production lines. Shown here is a restored example of the R.11/40 two-tonner dating from 1932.

Derivatives of the R-type included the 'RP' twenty-seater 'Director' bus with a step-frame 13 ft 6 in wheelbase chassis, four-wheel brakes, and using the larger 19.2 hp engine. Only 158 of these public service vehicles were made during the production period, 1932 and 1933. Major fleet users of the Director bus were East Kent and Aldershot & District.

Following the First World War the War Office, mindful of the need for suitable vehicles in the event of a future conflict, had a 'subvention' scheme in operation where fleet owners could claim an annual subsidy of £120 per vehicle for commercials made to a War Department specification, which called for a six-wheeler capable of carrying a useful load of 30 cwt on roads and 20 cwt cross-country. The specification also included a system of suspension where the rear driving wheels would bear equal weight under any conditions without twisting the springs or displacing the chassis. A standard form of rear bogie and suspension was designed by the Mechanical Transport Department of the War Office and manufacturers were offered the option of this or their own design matching this performance.

Using the War Office designed rear bogie, Morris Commercial introduced the 6 x 4 D-type six-wheeler in the second half of 1926 which followed the general lines of the Z-type commercial but with twin rear wheels on the two driven rear axles, and provision for removable tracks. Following military trials at Chobham Ridges test site, orders were placed with the Soho firm to equip first the Indian Army and later the British Army. Military versions normally had open cabs with canvas tilts, while those sold to civilian operators were fitted with cabs.

Details of the removable tracks for the rear wheels on the D-type six-wheeler. When not in use the tracks were stowed on the running boards.

The versatility of the War Office designed twin rear bogie suspension is demonstrated in this photograph of the D-type Morris Commercial under test.

One of the few surviving examples of the Morris Commercial D-type six-wheelers used by the British Army. This one was found derelict in an orchard and completely restored to military specification.

The Morris Commercial D-type six-wheeler continued in production until superseded in 1932, during which period alterations in design and numerous alternative specifications were available. A number of fire engines, for example, were built on the six-wheeler chassis. After the first 2,000 or so chassis the bogie centres were increased from 36 in to 40 in and an alternative to the original 10 ft wheelbase was the longer 12 ft wheelbase model. Subsidized by the Government of India, Morris Commercial produced an 'India type' with single wide low-pressure tyres. Similar chassis were also supplied to the Royal Air Force fitted with ambulance bodywork.

Another military use for the D-type six-wheeler was as an ambulance, such as this example supplied to the Royal Air Force.

Morris Commercial D-type six-wheelers were fitted out as wireless vans by the Marconi Wireless Telegraph Co. Ltd in the late 1920s. (The Marconi Company Ltd)

A few special six-wheelers were made by Morris Commercial. Illustrated here is the '4/5-seater six-wheeled touring car' specially constructed for the Prince of Wales (later King Edward VIII) for his African hunting trip.

For fire brigades these special versions, catalogued as Type-FD, were equipped as fire engines. Equipment supplied included a Gwynne two-stage turbine-type pump driven by a separate shaft from the engine, 2,000 ft of delivery hose, 40 ft of suction hose, a 120 ft hose reel, and a 30 ft extension ladder.

Unlike the D-type, which had a four-cylinder engine, the Morris Commercial Type-6D saloon was powered by six cylinders. Very few of these were manufactured and even fewer would have gone into private ownership. Most of the production went to the inter-war British Army for use as officers' staff cars.

Another six-wheeler of the period was the Morris Commercial RD-type bulk load carrier based on the R-type. As the name suggests, these vehicles were intended to carry light but bulky commodities, exemplified by Lyons Tea who had a number of van versions in their fleet. Only the forward of the twin rear axles were driven, the rear axle trailing. Between 1930 and 1932, 939 of these RD-types were built.

The engine used in the 6D-type was a 4256 cc unit rated at 26.8 hp. This view from the rear shows the partition behind the driver and the remainder of the seating accommodation. Note the wood slats on the petrol tank giving protection from loose stones. The step on the left facilitated easy entry from the rear door.

A mobile animal dispensary, based on the Morris Commercial RD-type bulk load carrier, was used by the People's Dispensary for Sick Animals in the 1930s.

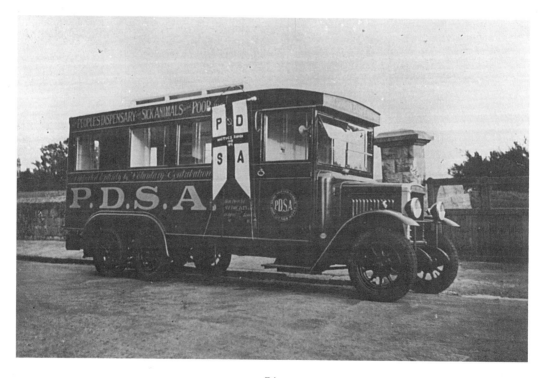

Although most previous commercials had been adapted when required as a public service vehicle, it was not until the early 1930s that purpose-built Morris Commercial bus chassis were available. The first of these was the 'Viceroy', or Y-type, normal control model powered by a six-cylinder side-valve 4256 cc engine. Coach and bus bodies were fitted to the Viceroy chassis by some of the many specialist bodybuilders of the period. One of the largest users of the Viceroy was the East Kent fleet, who favoured the Harrington and Beadle twenty-seater bodywork. At least one of the 272 Y-type chassis produced between 1930 and 1932 was used as a fire engine in Lancashire.

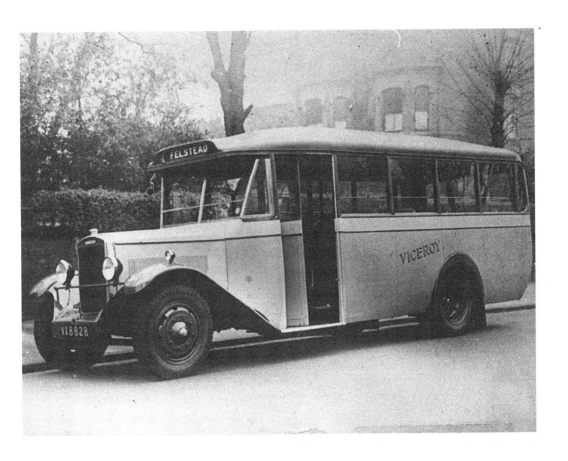

When Charles K. Edwards joined Morris Commercial Cars early in 1929, his experience with the London General Omnibus Co. was soon evident when the H-type 'Dictator' and the HD-type 'Imperial' buses were introduced. A unique feature of these models was the patented arrangement of the engine–gearbox–front axle unit which, to facilitate servicing, could be wheeled away from the chassis proper by means of a special skid supplied (see above). The engine itself, a six-cylinder inclined ohv unit, had some unusual and ingenious features such as the ability to remove the cylinder head without disturbing the valve timing or camshaft drive.

The Dictator, available as a normal control or forward control model with a wheelbase of just over 16 ft, or as a normal control 18 ft wheelbase version, was listed between 1930 and 1933. By 1933 some 133 units had been produced.

The Stewart & Ardern demonstrator is shown opposite (above) contrasting in size with the contemporary 1931 '£100' Morris Minor.

The first, and last, attempt by Sir William Morris to capture some of the lucrative double-decker bus market was with the 'Imperial' HD-type Morris Commercial. That this was an unsuccessful venture is indicated by the total build figure of eighty-three, sold between 1932 and 1933. Using the same pull-out engine as the Dictator, albeit bored-out to increase the capacity, the Imperial was offered in forward control drive only on a 16 ft 1 in wheelbase chassis. More than half of the Imperials made went to Birmingham Corporation, while most of the remainder (bodied by Park Royal) were taken by the East Kent fleet. Amazingly, one has survived the ravages of time and is awaiting restoration in the Birmingham area.

During the production period of these buses, and often using similar or modified parts of these PSVs, a small number of heavy-duty lorries were manufactured, an example being the K-type eight-tonner, which made use of the Dictator bus chassis and six-cylinder engine. Only a handful of these were produced, one of which was used by Morris Motors Ltd at Cowley to transport engines from their Coventry engine plant. A second is known to have been purchased by Moreland & Sons of 'England's Glory' match fame (above), while a third, with tanker body, was commissioned by Duckhams Oils.

Produced in larger numbers, or to be exact 112 units between 1931 and 1934, was the J-type 'Courier' in forward control rated at 5 tons, or 4 tons with normal control. Again the six-cylinder engine from the Dictator bus was employed and, like the bus, the power unit and front axle were arranged to wheel out for servicing.

On the left of the photograph below, taken in Morris Commercial's West Works in the early 1930s, Dictator chassis can be seen being assembled. The commercial chassis on the right are for the P-type 'Leader'.

The four-cylinder engined P-type or 'Leader' – a name which was later to be used on a completely different model – was made in larger quantities in both normal and forward control. Introduced in 1930, these heavy commercials were initially rated at 2$\frac{1}{2}$ tons but later uprated to a three-tonner. By 1934, when the model was phased out, 1,304 P-types had left the Adderley Park production lines.

Morris Commercial Cars Co. were quick to take advantage of a change in 1927 to the regulations governing the design of taxi-cabs. This was a particularly opportune time as a wide-track version of the Morris Oxford motor car, made by Morris Commercial and intended for the Empire market, had not been a success. Using this 'Empire Oxford' as a basis, the company introduced the first of the Morris Commercial taxis known as the Type-G International Taxi-Cab in 1929. Using the Z-type 15.9 hp four-cylinder engine, the taxi had an overhead worm rear axle giving a high ground clearance, a wide 58 in track, and a turning circle of 24 ft 9 in to comply with the Public Carriage Office test. About 840 of these International cabs were sold between 1929 and 1932.

Although Morris Commercial had been the first large British motor manufacturer to enter the taxi-cab market, the Austin taxi that followed it in 1930 was to prove the more popular and soon became an accepted part of the London traffic scene. Morris, nevertheless, continued to produce taxi-cabs and the successor to the original International model was the G2 Junior. Introduced in 1932, it made use of the well-tried 13.9 hp Morris side-valve engine then in use in the 1 ton truck. Two years later a six-cylinder version, the G2S Junior Six, was also listed; powered by the same 1938 cc engine as the contemporary Morris Fifteen-Six motor car.

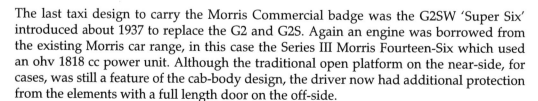
The last taxi design to carry the Morris Commercial badge was the G2SW 'Super Six' introduced about 1937 to replace the G2 and G2S. Again an engine was borrowed from the existing Morris car range, in this case the Series III Morris Fourteen-Six which used an ohv 1818 cc power unit. Although the traditional open platform on the near-side, for cases, was still a feature of the cab-body design, the driver now had additional protection from the elements with a full length door on the off-side.

With the outbreak of the Second World War in 1939, production came to an end. Its replacement, after the war, was the Wolseley Oxford.

Early in 1933, with Morris Commercial Cars now concentrating their production facilities at Adderley Park, Birmingham, a programme of rationalization took place and a new broad range of vehicles called the C-type was announced. Basically, the C-type covered capacity ratings between 30 cwt and 5 tons, with numerous body types such as vans, trucks, tippers, etc., and a high percentage of common parts were used throughout the range. Type designations consisted of letters and figures which indicated the wheelbase and capacity, for example the C.11/30 denoted a C-type vehicle with an 11 ft wheelbase (in rounded up figures) and a capacity of 30 cwt. To avoid an unwieldy '100 cwt' on the largest of the models, the figure 5 for tons was used.

Initially six-cylinder models were introduced having a common type of 25 hp side-valve engine, but within a short time a four-cylinder version was available; these having a longer stroke 24.8 hp power unit.

Illustrated here is a C-type normal control van dated 1936.

A long-wheelbase normal control C-type tipper truck in use in Lancashire, around 1934.

A 1934 ambulance version of the Morris Commercial C-type. The single rear wheels suggest that a CS.11/30 chassis had been used.

In addition to the conventional vans and trucks, the C-type was also used as the basis of more specialist vehicles such as this six-cylinder fire engine which went into service with the City of Worcester fire brigade in 1934. (K. Martin)

Another variation is this surviving example of a shooting brake, with bodywork by Mann Edgerton on the 30 cwt four-cylinder C.11/30 chassis built in 1934. (K. Martin)

Streamlined coach based on the 2 ton C-type chassis, supplied by Dominion Motor Ltd of New Zealand.

In addition to the choice of four- or six-cylinder engine, and a wide variation of load ratings, the C-type owner also had the option of a normal control or forward control vehicle. The C-type range also introduced a purpose-built 3 ton tractor unit for articulated six-wheelers, which were intended for coupling to trailers made by certain approved manufacturers such as Eagle, Taskers, Dyson, Brockhouse, Carrimore, etc. The C.9/60 tractor unit and Tasker trailer shown here is the restored ensemble owned by D. Stark of Durham.

Forward control variations of the C-type were available in 30 cwt, 2 ton and 3 ton ratings, with both four- or six-cylinder power units. They type designation of these would have the suffix letter F. Design and space considerations made the use of a gravity feed petrol supply, as used on the normal control models, unfeasible. Fuel supply on the forward control models was via an Autovac unit from a petrol tank mounted on the side of the chassis.

The 3 ton forward control C-type illustrated was in use in Lancashire in 1934. Its load of raw cotton in bales reflects the main local industry at the time.

The disposition of instruments and controls on the C-type forward control. Note the recessed dash, making the most of the driver's restricted space.

A smaller example of the forward control four-cylinder C-type. This restored model is the 30 cwt version, easily recognizable by the single wheels at the rear. All the larger models in the C-type range had double wheels on the rear axle.

Another forward control 30 cwt C-type. The special bodywork was the work of Bonnalack for the Borough of Poplar, Electricity Department.

A Morris Commercial C-type 'Leader' 4 ton van when new in 1935.

C-type removal vans in the fleet of Bishop & Sons, London. The rearmost vehicle is a T-type one-tonner, while the small van on the left in the background is a Morris 5 cwt Minor van. (R. Bishop)

A Singapore Volunteer Corps troop carrier based on the normal control C-type. Its subsequent history can only be guessed at, but no doubt it fell into the hands of the Japanese after Singapore fell in 1942.

The C-type formula, using the same basic design with many interchangeable components over a large range of ratings and sub-divided into four- and six-cylinder engines, was obviously a success for Morris Commercial. They repeated the idea when the C range was superseded by the 'CV' models around November 1937.

These new CV models carried the name 'Equi-load', which denoted a design said to ensure that the load and braking stresses were equally distributed between the two axles. Initially the Equi-load range comprised the larger CV-types covering 30 cwt to 5 tons, and the smaller 25 cwt LC model (presumably an abbreviation for 'light commercial'). As with their predecessors the new range used the same coding to indicate the wheelbase and capacity. Thus 'CVS.13/3' would denote a CV-type with a six-cylinder engine, a 13 ft wheelbase and a 3 ton rating. Similar four- and six-cylinder side-valve engines to those used in the C-type were employed for the CV models, but for the smaller LC a 15.9 hp ohv unit was used.

One of the larger six-cylinder forward control CVF.13/5 trucks is shown here.

These sacks of hops being loaded in Kent, in around 1946, form a large, bulky load for the forward control long-wheelbase CV-type Morris Commercial.

On the new CV-types the traditional perpendicular chromium-plated radiator shell gave way to a new, more rounded, black finished pressing, well forward of the front axle. Gone too was gravity feed for the fuel supply; all CV models utilized an Autovac, with the petrol tank mounted on the off-side chassis frame. Twin rear wheels were the norm for all but the smallest 30 cwt (CV.9/30 and CV.11/30) and the LC models.

One specialized version in the CV range was the six-cylinder engined, 11 ft wheelbase, ambulance based on a special ambulance chassis. Particular attention had been given to the suspension and to this end wide 900–16 extra low pressure tyres on disc wheels were fitted. Two versions were available, the Standard model and the De Luxe model, shown above. However, as the main differences between the two were in the type of equipment and fittings, no changes to the external appearance were obvious. Standard equipment included 'Purdah' glass windows each side and in the rear doors, extractor ventilators in the roof, full width well-step in the body complemented with a folding step, and Maltese or Red Cross lamp above the windscreen.

A less expensive 'Industrial' ambulance was also available based on the 9 ft LC 25 cwt van which had large, frosted drop windows each side of the body and similar frosted glass in each door.

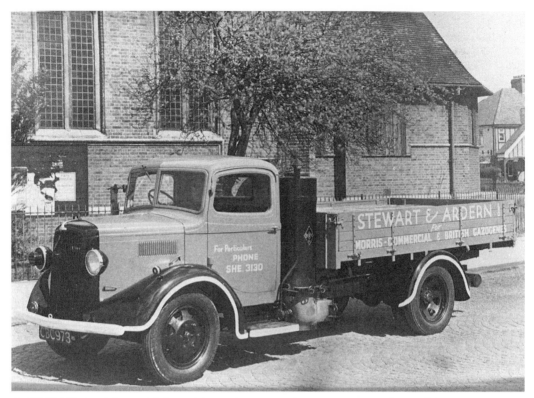

A CV.11/40 normal control drop-side truck converted to run on gas using a Gasagene converter during the Second World War. The headlamp masking and white lines on the extremities of the vehicle were obligatory during the war, the latter to assist visibility during the blackout.

Forward control CVF-type fire engine dating from 1948. This particular machine was in service with a Braintree (Essex) hospital until 1980. It is now in the hands of a Morris enthusiast.

Another CV-based fire engine is this surviving example of a Morris Commercial–Merryweather unit based on the six-cylinder 13 ft wheelbase $4\frac{1}{2}$ ton chassis.

Towards the end of the Second World War a few CV trucks were allowed to be produced for the home market using special Ministry of Supply licences. These had a utility specification and a notable feature of their appearance was the very small headlamps. Once Morris Commercial production got into its stride in 1946, the CV and LC models were again available, albeit only with four-cylinder engines. On the post-war version of the LC 25/30 cwt van the previously hinged doors on the cabs had now been changed to sliding doors, and these vans were soon to be seen throughout the country in GPO livery.

The driver's cab and controls in the pre-war Morris Commercial 25 cwt LC van. (P. Seymour)

A Morris Commercial 25 cwt LC van used by the London Midland & Scottish railway for parcel deliveries in 1946.

A restored example of the 25 cwt LC3 van. This particular vehicle was new in 1951. The LC3 version was the last of the LC series to have 20 in diameter wheels. On its successor, the LC4, the wheel size was reduced to 16 in diameter, albeit slightly wider. (J. Lowrie)

Production of the LC 25/30 cwt-type resumed after the war and continued in production until 1948. This model had a 9 ft 9 in wheelbase. Its successor, the LC3 (there was no 'LC2' model), as truck or van, was the same basic design, with the 2050 cc ohv engine, but a shorter 9 ft 6 in wheelbase. Eighteen and a half thousand LC3 models were produced. The illustration here is of a Morris Commercial LC3 in use as a hearse in Malaysia. (P. Seymour)

The LC4 version, which came on the scene in mid-1952, had a revised wheelbase of 10 ft 1 in and smaller diameter wheels shod with 7.50–16 tyres. Both van and truck versions were listed. The last of the series, the LC5, was introduced in May 1953. This had a larger four-cylinder petrol engine of 2199 cc, but was offered in truck form only. Another version, the LC05, with a four-cylinder 3400 cc diesel engine was introduced in December 1954. Both petrol and diesel models finished production in early 1960. The 1½ ton LC5 truck is illustrated.

The outbreak of the Second World War brought a severe curtailment in the production of Morris Commercials. During the 'phoney war' period some vehicles were still being produced for the home market but after the Dunkirk evacuation the motor industry production was put to the war effort. A new light commercial called the 15/20 cwt PV (or parcels van) was not announced until after the war but, in fact, fifty-two of these had been produced in 1939 and early 1940. Using the same ohv 15.9 hp engine as the LC 25/30 cwt, the flat-fronted PV van had a traditional hardwood-framed body panelled with metal-skinned plywood, and doors to the cab which were the sliding type to give easy access for door-to-door deliveries.

Early models had a horizontally split windscreen on the driver's side which allowed the upper portion to be opened. On later models the two sections making up the windscreen were fixed. Various other modifications were to be introduced, including larger section tyres, before the model finally stopped production in 1953, by which time some 15,769 of the vans had been made.

The prototype of the 15/20 cwt PV van. The final production model differed in detail; for example, the design of the wheels, wheel arches, petrol tank filler, etc.

Truck and van bodies being assembled at Morris Commercial Cars Ltd Works, Adderley Park, Birmingham, in 1948

During the currency of the PV model a number were used by the County of Middlesex Ambulance Service, as 'sitting case' ambulances, although a stretcher was fitted on the near-side. All passenger seats were provided with seat belts or lap straps. The drivers of these ambulances nicknamed the vehicles 'ice-cream carts'. (M. Bailey)

Two unusual variations on the PV chassis are these trucks with bodywork by a Danish coach-builder (above) and by a Swiss coachbuilder (below).

The 'NV' series followed the general styling of the LC5 but on a larger scale. These normal control trucks were first available as the NVS.12/3 three-tonner and the NVS.13/5 five-tonner in October 1950, both versions powered by six-cylinder 4197 cc ohv petrol engines. A few months later an optional 4459 cc six-cylinder Saurer diesel engine became available for the five-tonner as the NVO.13/5.

An additional three-tonner, with a smaller four-cylinder side-valve petrol engine of 3770 cc, was on offer from September 1953 as the NV.12/3, and yet another variation came in 1954 with the introduction of the NVO.13/5. This truck had a 3.4 litre diesel engine.

Short wheelbase, 5 ton tippers, with either the six-cylinder Saurer diesel engine or an ohv 4197 cc petrol engine, as NVO.11/5 and NVS.11/5 respectively, had a production run from 1953 to 1955 when, together with the three-tonners, the NV models were phased out. The longer 13 ft 9 in wheelbase five-tonners had ceased production the previous year.

One other vehicle to use the NVS chassis was the ambulance. With a six-cylinder petrol engine of 4197 cc, the 12 ft wheelbase chassis was purpose-designed with low pressure 9.25–16 tyres and large telescopic shock-absorbers front and rear to ensure vibration-free running. The actual ambulance bodies were built by various proprietary bodybuilders such as Appleyards of Leeds, Wadham Brothers of Hampshire and Kennings Ltd of Derbyshire.

Morris Commercial 12 ft wheelbase 5 ton FVS.12/5 of 1950.

The five-tonners in the 'FV' series of Morris Commercials can be considered the forward control contemporaries of the various NV-type normal control trucks, although the earliest examples of the former were available as early as 1948. The FV models underwent considerable variations during their production span.

First on the scene was the FVO.12/5, which was a 12 ft wheelbase truck with a six-cylinder 4256 cc diesel engine. This made its debut in May 1948 and was followed in October of the same year by a 3770 cc four-cylinder petrol version, the FV.12/5. Tippers with a shorter 9 ft wheelbase (FV.9/5 and FVO.9/5) were also available at the same time.

The 5 ton trucks were superseded in January 1953 with a new six-cylinder 4197 cc ohv petrol and a 4459 cc diesel version as FVS.12/5 and FVSO.12/5 respectively. The following year both of these had been re-styled with the new Series II cab. This new style cab, with narrower forward-hinged doors, allowed the driver to reverse more easily. Another feature was the opening quarter-lights. The windscreen was arranged so that either half could be opened independently and secured in any desirable position. This new cab was also used for the 7 ft tractor unit FVS.7/5 and the FVO.7/5 dating from late 1953 until March 1955.

The prime movers first appeared in 1950 with the FV.9/5, which had a four-cylinder petrol engine of 3770 cc, and the six-cylinder FVO.9/5. The latter was initially powered by a 4256 cc diesel engine but was soon replaced by a larger 4459 cc unit. Morris Commercial recommended the use of the Scammell trailer with the prime movers.

The new style Series II cab introduced on the FVS.12/5 in 1954.

The 5 ton Morris Commercial truck, FVO.12/5, was available from May 1948 until January 1953. Early models were powered by a six-cylinder Saurer diesel engine built under licence. A Morris-designed diesel engine was later fitted.

An articulated unit using the FVO.9/5 diesel prime mover mated to a 20 ft Tasker trailer. Dating from 1949, this example would have been powered by the 4256 cc six-cylinder Saurer engine, and was used in Scotland to haul heavy pre-cast concrete products.

First introduced at the Commercial Transport Show, Earls Court, in October 1948 (although it did not go into full production until a year later), the new forward control J-type 10 cwt van could have been considered the replacement for the Morris Series Y 10 cwt van from Cowley, particularly as like the latter its engine was off-set to the nearside. (On right-hand drive vehicles that is. Left-hand drive vans had the off-set to the right – hence the need for two starting-handle holes at the base of the radiator grille.) However, for reasons better known to Morris Commercial and Morris Motors management, they tended to compete in the small-capacity van market. The true successor to the Series Y van was the normal control 10 cwt van based on the Morris Oxford car which appeared on the scene in May 1950. The new J-type Morris Commercial followed the trend for light commercials, with sliding doors on both sides at the front and rear doors with outrigger hinges allowing the doors to open against the sides.

A Morris Commercial J-type van still in use for the sale of ice-cream in Somerset. (M. Plummer)

In February 1957 the J-type became the JB-type 'express delivery van' when a larger ohv engine was introduced with four-speed gearbox, replacing the earlier side-valve/three-speed gearbox unit. They were to find favour with the General Post Office and considerable numbers joined their fleet as postal, telephone engineers' and radio detector vans. As with all Morris vehicles supplied to the GPO up to that time, the specification differed from the civilian versions. Externally, these differences included rubber wings, separate head and side lamps, front and rear bumpers, fog lamp bracket, and various security locking devices. On later models opening windscreens were fitted.

Early in its production run, a subtle change was made when the badge was altered from 'Morris Commercial' to read simply 'Morris'. By this time the Austin–Morris amalgamation had resulted in the formation of the British Motor Corporation and this change might have been a prelude to future 'badge engineered' models.

Shown here is a Morris Commercial JB-type which had been in service with the GPO in 1960.

In 1960 a new redesigned vehicle rated at 10 cwt, in van or pick-up form, was launched as the J4, badged as either 'Morris' or 'Austin', with a variation in grille design to provide a cosmetic difference. This model was redesignated as the J4-M10 in 1961 when they became available with a choice of petrol or diesel 1.5 litre engines, and subsequently, in 1968, sold simply as the BMC J4.

To add to the proliferation of models, Morris Commercial had earlier, in June 1956, added a 15 cwt version of the J-type, with single-piece windscreen, known as the J2. This model had a four-cylinder ohv petrol engine and was offered as a light van, a pick-up, or a minibus. The introduction of an optional 1489 cc diesel engine coincided, in 1961, with a change of name to the 'J2–M16'. Later a 1622 cc diesel engine appears to have been an option.

Illustrated is a Morris J4-M10 series van as used by the GPO.

The forward control 'LD' series of Morris Commercials filled a gap in the early 1950s for a 1 ton, and later a 1½ ton, delivery van. The LD had a metal-panelled 235 cu ft van body with a wooden plank floor and further timber was introduced as strips to provide internal protection for the body sides. Wide rear doors, a low floor line and sliding doors at the front facilitated on–off loading. As first introduced in July 1952, with a four-cylinder 2199 cc ohv engine, the radiator grille was of an inverted heart shape with slightly protruding headlamps either side. After the first 3,243 vehicles had been produced, the front end treatment was changed to incorporate a wide, horizontal radiator grille and headlamps which were recessed, and the 'Morris Commercial' badge was replaced by one simply denoting the make as 'Morris'. This change in frontal design coincided, in January 1955, with the alternative diesel-engined version called the LD01 shown below.

In April 1960 both models were fitted with four-speed synchromesh gearboxes and ,although the appearance remained much the same, they were renamed 'LD4' for the petrol version and 'LD-M20'

Twelve months after the introduction of the original one-tonner, Morris Commercial offered a 1½ ton version. Seemingly identical in design to the LD1, careful examination would have revealed an overall length increase of about 7 in and a more arched roof to give the van increased capicity. To cater for the extra load a heavier rear axle was fitted together with stronger springs and larger tyres. This 1½ ton van was given the identity 'LD2'. Production ran from October 1953. The various changes made to the one-tonner also applied to the LD2, making it the LD5 and LD05, then later in 1961 the 'LD-M30'.

Until the introduction of the Series III forward control series of trucks, starting in March 1955, Morris Commercial cabs had always had, at the very least, a vestige of the old type Morris radiator shell and consequently the frontal appearance of the forward control cabs were aesthetically balanced. This could not be said of the 'FE' cab on Series III vehicles which, with the introduction of a lower horizontal grille, left a considerable blank area between it and the windscreen, giving the impression of a tall cab. This impression was moderated when fleet owners added their own livery markings to the front and the doors.

Technological and cost restraints were still dictating the use of flat glass and this was reflected in the windscreen design on the FE cab, which comprised two separate and equal size frames, albeit hinged at the top.

Four basic ratings were offered, starting with the 3 ton '303.FC' model on an 11 ft 6 in wheelbase, giving an option of six-cylinder ohv petrol engine of 3993 cc, or a four-cylinder 3.4 litre diesel. The same diesel engine powered the larger four-tonner '503.FC' which came on the market a month later. Next in rating was the 5 ton '503.FC', which was alternatively a 13 ft 4 in wheelbase truck or a short wheelbase version (10 ft) tipper, both offered with a six-cylinder petrol or 5.1 litre diesel. The longest of the series was the 701 seven-tonner, 5.1 litre diesel power unit only, with power steering and an Eaton two-speed axle as standard. There followed in March 1955 a short wheelbase version (12 ft 6 in), and an even shorter 10 ft wheelbase tipper was listed the following year. ·

All the Series III forward control models were superseded in late 1959 by the new 'FG' series.

A 3 ton forward control Series III Morris Commercial with the FE design cab.

93

Typical of the Series III Morris Commercials was this 3 ton diesel engined 303.FC used by Minns (Oxford) Ltd in 1956.

This larger 7 ton 701 was operated by E.G. Stead & Son Ltd of Shropshire in 1957.

The 701 truck.

The smaller of the FG trucks, the 1¹/₂ ton, was phased in to replace the LC variations. First introduced early in 1960, the FG series were based on a revolutionary forward control design officially known as 'angle-planning' but soon getting the nickname 'three-penny bits', from the small coin with twelve flat sides. The hinged doors on the new cab were cut back so that when fully open they projected no more than 2 in beyond the width of the truck platform. Another feature of the design was the low set corner windows giving extra vision range, especially when manoeuvering.

With their Morris badge, the 30 cwt trucks were known as the FG 1¹/₂ ton, renamed FG.K30 in 1962 (when production was moved to Bathgate, Scotland), and later, in 1968, as the 360.FG when the gross vehicle weight rather than the payload was used for classification. Austin versions were initially called the 30 cwt S.200 F/C truck. A choice of the 2.2 litre four-cylinder ohv petrol or a diesel engine could be fitted.

The first diesel engined version of the FG.K30 made at Bathgate is preserved and may be seen at the Transport Museum, Kelvin Hall, Glasgow.

Also within the FG series were the FG.K40 2 ton truck, the FG.K60 3 ton truck, the 4 ton FG.K80, and the larger FG.K100 rated at 5 tons.

The Morris Commercial FG.K30 truck.

The FG.K30 shown here clearly illustrates the 'threepenny bit' cab with its cut back doors. The contortion required to change gear behind the driver's seat was soon mastered.

The 2.2 litre four-cylinder ohv petrol engine used in the 1¹/₂ ton FG trucks.

The WE series of Morris Commercial trucks was produced for operators with a preference for normal control cabs. The smaller of the series, the WE.K30 (originally T.200) and WE.K40 (originally T.203), were initially available in the early 1960s only for the export market, but were later, in 1964, released for the home market, by which time it had a redesigned cab (WF) with twin headlamps and a single-piece windscreen replacing the earlier arrangement of two separate frames.

The normal control three-tonner went through numerous changes from the time of its introduction in March 1955 as the Series III '303.NC' model, with a six-cylinder ohv petrol engine or a 3.4 litre diesel fitted with the WE cab – a development of the Austin cab from the Loadstar range; the rear portion being virtually pure Austin. In 1962 the description was changed to WE.K60 and in common with many of the heavy Morris Commercials was being produced at Bathgate. A larger 3.8 litre diesel engine replaced the earlier type in December 1963 and by July the following year the redesigned WF cab, with twin headlamps and a one-piece windscreen, was being fitted, and soon gained the nickname of the 'Woofer'.

The five-tonner normal control followed a similar development route, starting off as the Series III 503.NC, becoming the WE.K100 in January 1962, then in July 1964 being fitted with the Woofer (WF) cab. The 6 ton WE.K120 was also fitted with the WF cab about the same time. Prime movers with the WE cab included the WE.K240 and the WE.K300 (1961 to 1964).

The smaller versions of the WE series had the option of a 4 litre six-cylinder petrol engine or four-cylinder diesels in either 3.4 or 3.8 litre. For the larger five- and six-tonners only diesel engines were fitted, being six-cylinder 5.1 or 5.7 litres, driving through four- or five-speed gearboxes and the optional Eaton two-speed rear axle. On all models hydraulic shock absorbers and dual windscreen wipers were deemed extras.

Many of the WE vehicles were sold to African countries, particularly Nigeria, as the brakes were not considered to be up to the UK specification.

The WE.K100 5 ton chassis was used as the basis for the works' fire engine by the MG Car Company Ltd at Abingdon. Equipment included a 400 gallon Godiva pump.

FH.K140 7 ton forward control tipper.

Recognition of the 7 and 8 ton FF and FH models is made easy by the cosmetic chromium-plated surround on the grille. This was not fitted to the 'smaller' 5 ton models.

The FH models were to prove something of an interim arrangement between the FF and the FJ tilt-cab – probably better known to heavy goods drivers as the 'G-cab'.

The forward control cab design would appear to have been an important selling point in the mid-1950s. As already mentioned, the features of the curious 'threepenny bit' cab allowed the driver to make a swift and easy entry, while any manoeuvering into warehouse bay or goods yard was simplified by the low-set corner windows. The new style 'FF' cab, introduced in 1958 for the larger Morris Commercials, was given as much publicity as the performance of the actual vehicles. This was an all-steel cab with a canopied wrap-round windscreen, broad rear windows and twin exterior mirrors to aid reversing. Provision for a fitted radio was made and the appropriate equipment was an optional extra. 'Throughout every journey', said the publicity, 'the driver and mate get comfort travel in an all-steel cab which has relaxing upholstery on fully adjustable seats, dust and draught sealing, and provision for heater and radio.' Asbestos lining on the manifold side of the engine cowling panels would certainly not be a selling point today.

A modification of the FF cab called the 'FH' was externally unchanged but was necessary to cater for the beneath floor mounting of the six-cylinder diesel engine on the FH.K100, FH.K140 and the FH.K160. In 1962 Halmo Engineering Co. of Midlothian went a step further in increasing driver comfort by modifying the FF cab to the 'FF Halmo Crew Cab', where the rear of the Morris cab was cut off completely and a coachbuilt section, including a third door, was inserted between the two parts. The same swagging of the forward control cab was used and the floor and engine tunnel section was coachbuilt into position. The additional crew cab was also suitable for use as a sleeping compartment.

FJ models were the last of the commercials to carry the 'Morris' badge. In August 1968 it was announced that the distributor set-up had been drastically pruned down from 223 Austin and Morris Commercial outlets to 141 to handle BMC vehicles, as all the commercials would henceforth be called. 'Badge engineering' had finished, the BMC name would be used on all vehicles, together with the British Leyland symbol.

The FJ comprised not only a new tilt-cab design but a new chassis frame. As with the previous FH models the diesel engines were mounted at an angle of 29 degrees in the chassis beneath the cab floor.

Designed by Graham Ibbotson, the FJ had problems from the outset. At Bathgate investment had been made in new machine tools so engine production was transferred to the Scottish works, and at the same time the opportunity was taken to lengthen the engine block by approximately $5/8$ in to give more space between the liners. To do this the cylinder bores were altered from an arrangement of two banks of three bores, as had been made by Morris Commercial Cars, to three banks of two bores. Despite the fact that the 5.1 and 5.7 litre units used in the FH were reliable, when fitted to the new FJ they suffered badly from overheating. A significant factor was a vertical radiator used on the FH, whereas the new FJ used a cross-flow type and dispersal of airlocks was not easy. Another problem was caused when the Bathgate machine operators found difficulty in holding the tolerance where, in order to obtain a good gasket seal, the liners had to stand

This FF.K140 seven-tonner used by C.A. King & Sons of Andover in the late months of 1958 illustrates the identical external appearance of the FH and FF cabs. As a sign of things to come the letters BMC were already appearing above the name 'Morris' on the badge.

One of the last Morris badged commercials, the FJ 7 ton refrigerated van with underfloor diesel engine.

proud of the block face by 0.002 in to 0.006 in, in addition to being more or less consistent for all six liners. The problem proved serious and costly. Some engines went out with the liners below the face of the block and as a result gasses entered the cooling system, air-locks occurred, and the engines boiled. Engines were being replaced under warranty all over the world.

The FJ gained a bad reputation and attempts to solve the problem by re-naming the vehicle the 'Laird', and then the 'Boxer', and introducing modifications, did not mend the damage done to the image. The Boxer used the 5.1 litre engines in a vertical position and apart from a slight bump to accommodate the top of the engine, a flat floor was still achieved, indicating that the complication of the angled underfloor mounting and a cross-flow radiator was not necessary in the first place.

5·7 DIESEL ENGINE
(UNDERFLOOR)

Early Morris Commercial Cars' version of the troublesome 5.7 litre underfloor diesel engine.

Morris Commercial FJ chassis with the tilt cab.